TREE PITHY POINTS

Brief messages on tree biology, tree care, and philosophy

by

Alex L. Shigo, Ph.D.

Former chief scientist, U.S. Forest Service

Front Cover – Center of a red oak
When you look deep enough, you will find a star in every person.

Back Cover – Mycorrhizae on birch

Shigo and Trees, Associates
P.O. Box 769
Durham, NH 03824

PREFACE

Tree talks have been a major part of my life since 1960. I have kept slides to a minimum, and never used a note on stage. Preparation for a talk always meant writing brief messages on yellow pads. This book contains a selection of some of these messages. They are numbered only for easy reference. Start any place in the book and read a few. Then think about them.

THANKS

Dr. Kevin Smith, Plant Physiologist, U.S. Forest Service, for reviewing the manuscript.

TREE PITHY POINTS

1. The best way to roll a good snowball is to keep changing directions. Then you end with a ball and not a snow roll that falls over. This is the way I have developed these pithy points.

1.   The more you learn about what you are seeking, the better
      the chances are that you will find it.

      The bronze figure is reminding researchers to see and
      touch as they enter the wood products laboratory,
      Bundesanstalt für Materialprüfung, at Berlin-Dahlem,
      Germany.

2. Trees are plants that are perennial, woody, shedding, and compartmented. Trees usually have a single stem over three meters tall.

3. Cells are basic units of life.

4. Life is a state where parts and processes requiring energy are so highly ordered that they repeat.

5. Death is a state where parts and processes requiring energy become so disordered that they do not repeat.

6. Forests are systems where trees and many other communities of organisms are connected in ways that ensure high quality survival for all.

7. People who hate trees develop heartrot.

8. Trees that made the coal fields had spores, very little lignin, and usually a single meristem.

9. Modern trees have multiple growing points in the form of branches, lots of lignin in cell walls, and seeds.

10. Most trees came in groups.

11. Trees are the most massive, longest living, and tallest organisms ever to grow on earth.

12. Trees are living things that have defense processes and protection features.

13. Trees are generating systems. Animals are regenerating systems.

14. Trees do not move away from their problems.

15. Trees have woody and non-woody roots.

2.   Trees got their genetic codes while growing with many
     associates.

16. Mycorrhizae are organs made up of tree and fungus tissues. The organs facilitate the absorption of elements from the soil.

17. The symplast is a highly ordered three-dimensional connection of living protoplasm in trees.

18. The apoplast is the tough non-living framework that holds the symplast in place.

19. Compartmentalization is the tree's defense process where boundaries form that resist spread of infections and that defend the liquid transport, energy storage, and mechanical support systems.

20. Codit is a model of compartmentalization.

21. Bark is made up of an outer periderm and an inner phloem.

22. Periderm is made up of a phellogen, phelloderm, and phellem.

23. Phloem is a transport tissue where energy containing substances dissolved in liquids move from leaves toward non-woody roots.

24. Xylem is a transport tissue where elements essential for life, and other substances, move in liquids from non-woody roots toward leaves.

25. When xylem is lignified, it is called wood.

26. Wood is a highly ordered arrangement of living, dying, and dead cells that have walls of cellulose, hemicelluloses, and lignins.

3.   When we plant trees in cities, we should try to give them conditions that best serve their genetic codes.

27. Trees are big batteries.

28. Trees seal, not heal, wounds.

29. Photosynthesis is an energy-trapping process.

30. Respiration is an energy-releasing process.

31. Energy is a concept of forces that do work. Photosynthesis and respiration are two sides of the same coin.

32. Matter is a concept of particles that form substances.

33. Seeds are ripened ovules.

34. Fruits are ripened ovaries and their attached parts.

35. Boundaries define the limits of things.

36. Boundaries resist, not stop, the spread of things.

37. Most wounds do not lead to decayed wood or hollows.

38. Make pruning cuts as close as possible to the branch collars.

39. There are no data to show that wound dressings prevent or stall decay.

40. People who call fertilizers plant food should wash their mouths out with wound dressing.

41. Callus is undifferentiated, meristematic tissue that has very little lignin.

42. Woundwood is differentiated tissue that has lots of lignin.

43. Cellulose is a long twisting polymer of glucose units.

4.   As cities and home sites become more prosperous, people want more trees.

44. Hemicelluloses are polymers of shorter chains of sugars.

45. Lignins are complex three-dimensional polymers of phenol propane units.

46. Trees play games in the wind. Sometimes they get rough!

47. Ants live in trees and eat elsewhere.

48. Termites usually eat in trees and live elsewhere. (Some tropical termites live in nests on trees.)

49. Teak trees are square in cross section, when young.

50. Thou shall not cut or remove branch collars.

51. Thou shall not plant tall maturing trees in small spaces or under utility lines.

52. Thou shall not plant trees deeply!

53. Good tree people don't top trees.

54. Cladoptosis is branch shedding, and not related to bad breath.

55. Don't call tree mutilators, butchers. Butchers are highly skilled people.

56. When the tree fell on a computer, the bark silenced a lot of bytes!

57. The casparian strip is not a gambling zone.

58. Rhizobium gives nitrogen a fix in dark nodules.

59. "We must go metric," should be on signs about three by four feet.

5.   Some people want to be so close to trees that they design
       houses around them.

60. We need a society for all the lone pines.

61. If trees cannot move, how do they get ring shakes?

62. Yeast growing in sap from spring wounds provides a spring tonic for many organisms.

63. Remember, roots go down and trunks go up.

64. Spiders were the first on the web.

65. People who believe all roots are shallow should try pulling up a young sapling of beech, oak, or hickory.

66. If trees could talk, I'm sure they would yell out a four-letter word – HELP!

67. We need to bring Attila the Hun back to deal with people who hurt trees for money.

68. Trees make love quietly.

69. Trees connect living and dead cells in ways so that the dead parts still benefit the entire tree.

70. Think what happens to the person on the up side of a seesaw when the other person suddenly gets off when it is in the down position. Now you know what a tree feels like after overpruning.

71. Trees did pretty well before humans got here.

72. If trees died when mistreated, there would not be many trees around.

73. Grass and trees made an agreement years ago to stay in their own territories.

6.   People in the Orient train trees to grow in shapes they consider attractive.

74. Anybody can answer a question. But, is the answer correct?

75. Robots like lists and recipes.

76. Training without educating makes robots. Educating without training makes waste. Both, training and educating are needed.

77. When connections are broken, things won't work.

78. Communication is the ultimate connection.

79. Communication is the transmission of a message.

80. DNA is the message for new life.

81. Transmission means the receiver receives exactly what the sender sends.

82. Messages are information units so highly ordered that their content cannot be misunderstood.

83. Dry rot does not advance in dry wood.

84. Poplars are big plants hoping some day to become trees.

85. Certification means receiving a certificate that guarantees reliability, or the certifier endorses the actions of the one who is certified. Think about it!

86. Every person should read Plato's The Republic, and especially the story about the cave people.

87. Education cures ignorance.

88. Happiness is touching a tree while watching your family play with your dog.

7. People in north-central Spain correctly pollarded these
    London Plane trees, and then grafted all the top branches.

89. The pines of Rome are *Pinus pinea*.

90. A city without trees is dead.

91. Newton's apple fell from a tree and started classical physics.

92. When possible, plant trees in clusters.

93. Use more ecoart-nurse logs in landscapes.

94. Science uses one word for concepts that take pages to explain. In legalese, pages of words are used to explain one word.

95. Man's first responsibility was to care for the garden, (Genesis 2-15).

96. Adjustments to change come three ways: passion, money, legal. Passion – to do your best; Money – to save it or make it.; Legal – comply or else.

97. People who have all the answers don't take questions.

98. Education is a race toward higher states of ignorance.

99. The most beautiful flowers often grow in rocky soils and crevices.

100. Recognizing natural connections is the key to a fulfilling life.

101. You can connect a water line with a gas line. The water will taste funny and the stove won't work. When I see some landscapes, I think of this.

102. Sometimes I sit and think. Sometimes I just sit.

8. The shade given by this *Pinus pinea* in The Vatican is welcomed by the tired tourists. The construction protects the tree from injury.

103. In <u>Moby Dick</u>, a storm disrupted the compass. The sailor did not understand why Captain Ahab beat him when he said they were sailing rapidly homeward toward the west. The ship was sailing into the early morning sun. Common sense beats machines and devices every time.

104. There is nothing more daunting than a blank page.

105. You should not sit down to write. You should sit down to unload ideas already formed.

106. If some people could put rainbows in bottles and sell them, they would do it.

107. You cannot buy a quick cure to relieve ignorance.

108. Never insult your audience.

109. Speak up to be heard. Stand up to be seen. Shut up when your time is up to be appreciated.

110. Curiosity is the fuel for the machinery of life. Humor is the lubricant.

111. Food is a substance that provides an energy source and elements essential for life.

112. A thinking person outside of the establishment is dangerous.

113. Socrates' crime was that he started people thinking.

114. One thinking person asked, "Why are we told to 'deep feed' when we are also told that roots are shallow?" This person is dangerous.

115. My only guarantee is that you will still go away confused, but at a much higher level.

9. Trees not only provide beauty and shade, but they trap more of the sun's energy than any other organism, and pass it along to many communities of associates, including humans.

116. Would it not be wonderful if all the wonder products came with proof of efficacy?

117. If tree trunks on the inside were first viewed from the longitudinal radial plane, would the growth increments be called growth stripes?

118. Trees have indoor plumbing.

119. If you know what you are looking for, chances are good that you will find it.

120. Long before man can destroy the natural system, the system will destroy man.

121. Appearance and vigor are not related.

122. The gnarled and twisted trees that are still alive are vigorous. The less vigorous trees are gone.

123. You cannot have a subjective dependent variable. (But, it has been done!)

124. Without controls you have no experiment.

125. As survival pressures increase, individuals become smaller, and mature and reproduce at an earlier age.

126. Just because veneer-grade trees are decreasing in numbers does not mean trees are decreasing in vigor.

127. Vigor is the capacity to survive when threatened.

128. Vitality is the ability to grow under the conditions you find yourself.

129. Capacity is what you have – potential, savings. Ability is what you are doing with what you have – kinetic, buying things.

10.   Trees continue to support their soil associates by
supplying a rich source of carbon and other essential
elements as they drop leaves, twigs, branches, and finally
give their trunks and woody roots.

130. The second law of energy flow allows for no exceptions.

131. The second law states that any system to remain orderly must have a continuous supply of energy.

132. The laws of energy can be paraphrased as: You can never win, but only break even. You can only break even at absolute zero. You can never reach absolute zero. The answer to life is high quality time.

133. If the specs are wrong for doing the job, get them changed!

134. The responsibility of professional arborists is to give trees as much high quality time as possible.

135. Trees have dignity.

136. Dignity means to command respect.

137. Tree mutilation destroys a tree's dignity.

138. People who destroy the dignity of trees for money should be made to slide down the trunk of a tree, such as *Chorisia speciosa*, that has large, tough thorns.

139. Leaders are not afraid to make a decision, and ride it out.

140. People who believe that trees bleed must put maple blood on their pancakes.

141. Greedy people develop buttrot.

142. Consider the poor soul who thought the pericycle was a bicycle that only goes in circles.

143. Be kind to your critics. They spend a great amount of time working for you.

11.   Trees grow in many climates of the world. Where winters are cold, the above ground portions of the trees go dormant as they supercool. In many places, the below ground portions of the trees are very active in winter as they absorb elements essential for life.

144. The man who lost his keys in the swamp was looking for them inside a building because the light was better and it was nice and warm.

145. Teachers with closed minds are the most dangerous people in the world.

146. To teach is to learn.

147. It is not how much you know, but how much you know that is correct that makes you wise.

148. Knowledge is a measure of what you know. Wisdom is what you do with what you know that benefits survival.

149. Quality means the characteristics that describe a product or performance. Quality can be high or low. Some people have quality control for low quality.

150. If you think timing is not important, consider the fate of the person who asked the boss for a raise right before lunch, and on Monday yet!

151. People who prune the old-fashioned way should be made to go to an old-fashioned dentist.

152. Education and wages are twins that grow and mature at the same rate.

153. It is not your speed but your direction toward your goal that makes you successful.

154. Reach for 100 always, but sometimes it is wise to grab a 90 and run.

155. Natural systems operate on a basis of 80 plus or minus ten.

156. The misfits of today may be the fits of tomorrow.

12.   The soils that do not freeze in winter, or non-frozen soils beneath shallow frozen soils, are alive with many insects, bacteria, fungi, and small worms.

157.	Mozart used the same notes available to all the other composers. He wrote melodies that people could take with them.

158.	The note A from a violin and the same note from a trumpet both have the same number of vibrations. Nature works the same way. Think about it.

159.	The capacity to adjust to changes is nature's secret for survival.

160.	The growth of the chipping industries tells you something about the condition of our forest trees.

161.	Humpty-Dumpty said, a word means what he wants it to mean. Socrates said, just tell us what you want it to mean. Voltaire said, once we know this, there will be no arguments.

162.	What is plant food?

163.	New ideas and new babies need some cleaning before their true beauty shows.

164.	Can you imagine the Wright brothers trying to get approval today to fly their airplane?

165.	Walter Reed separated yellow fever from malaria, then both diseases were treated separately.

166.	What is the balance of nature? Balance is the equalization of opposing forces. Stop. Dead?

167.	Poor Copernicus and Galileo. We still say the sun rises and sets.

13.   These mycorrhizae flourished in soils below water that
      was covered by ice.

168. Copernicus said the Pope's job was to tell people how to get to heaven, and his job was to tell people how the heavens go. Nice try!

169. Nature presents variations. The theme is always there.

170. Modern Arboriculture is tree care based on an understanding of tree biology.

171. Chemistry is the science of the arrangement and resulting properties of atoms.

172. Atom One, "I think I just lost an electron." Atom Two, "Are you sure?" Atom One, "I'm positive."

173. All living things are bags of chemicals connected by electrical currents.

174. People who say they are against all chemicals apparently do not understand what that means.

175. Less than 1% of the insects and fungi are harmful to humans. Think about that when you use a product that kills everything.

176. Oxygen, carbon dioxide, and water are the actors in photosynthesis and respiration. They trap, transport, store, and supply energy and in the end they are still oxygen, carbon dioxide, and water.

177. Be a 300% person. Learn to do more than one thing at a time.

178. When trees are upright they are timber; when they are horizontal they are lumber.

14.   Mycorrhizae are organs made up of tree and fungus tissues. The organs facilitate the absorption of elements, especially large ions such as phosphate ions. Shown here is an endomycorrhiza that was growing in between dead leaves. The fungi grow within the tube-like organs of endomycorrhizae.

179. When Wayne Gretzky was asked about his success in hockey, he said he does not skate where the puck is, but where he thinks the puck will be.

180. The biggest organism in the ocean is not a fish.

181. The biggest birds, ostriches, do not fly.

182. When one part of a system becomes dominant, it leads the system.

183. Big fish eat little fish. Little microbes eat big fish.

184. Any time something moves, there is a cost.

185. Think. Exercise the mind.

186. First you learn to play an instrument. A few people then learn to play music.

187. I would rather dance and sing to a melody than march to some drummer near or far.

188. Some people get their conscience removed and then sell quick cures.

189. Most of the so-called lightning cracks shown to me were caused by Joe Lightning Tree Service.

190. Do people who say arbor i' culture say par li' a ment?

191. Would you go to a doctor who flunked anatomy?

192. Trees can have many "buds" and still be sober.

193. Long before gas chromatography, sailors knew the smell of rot in ships.

15.   In ectomycorrhizae, the fungi grow mainly in the outer cells of the organ. Often the hyphae of the fungi coat the organ and grow ten to twenty centimeters beyond. These hyphae not only greatly increase the absorbing capacity of the organ, but some of the hyphae may connect with other hyphae from mycorrhizae on trees of other species.

194. Life is a journey powered by the sun and formed by chemicals borrowed from earth. Death is the end of the journey when the borrowed chemicals are returned to be used for new life.

195. To understand the design of water is to recognize the existence of a designer.

196. People who do not read starve the mind.

197. The greatest teachers told stories.

198. Never interrupt a person who is telling a story.

199. Your dictionary should be your best friend.

200. If you have twenty things to do, and only time to do three, which do you do?

201. Biotic and abiotic often switch places.

202. Real climbers don't use spikes on living trees.

203. Defense means building a wall. Protection is the wall after it is built.

204. The ambitious guest (Hawthorne) said he wanted to leave something for others. What will you leave?

205. Curiosity is the beginning of a good life.

206. Learn to say "thank you" and "please" in the language of the country you are visiting and you will be welcomed.

207. Consider that you may be wrong.

208. When growth exceeds energy to maintain order, the system will fail.

16.   Mycorrhizae grow in abundance beneath and between decaying leaves and old logs. Tree roots with mycorrhizae are shown here in old decaying logs of eastern white pine.

209. Say a kind word for suberin the next time you uncork a fine bottle of wine. Also, bless the yeasts, which are fungi!

210. ETOH is ethanol that yeasts provide for one and all. Anaerobic respiration, take with care for recreation.

211. Trees respond rapidly when hit.

212. Trees have many associates — friends.

213. Trees do not live beyond their means.

214. We have no word for a substance that is both living and dead — wood, soil.

215. As rainbows get bigger, it gets more difficult to tell where one color ends and another begins.

216. Bacteria are very small. They do big things.

217. Robots do not get workman's compensation.

218. Why do so many things come in threes? Might it be that threes resist balance?

219. Roots do not "seek out" water.

220. Trees never knew stumps until axes and saws came.

221. Trees don't read textbooks.

222. Music exercises the soul. Running exercises the body. Reading exercises the mind.

223. Learning concepts is the same as learning to ride a bicycle; you never forget.

224. People and trees have roots. Root problems can affect both groups.

17.   This mycorrhiza was growing during winter in brown-rotted wood of an old white pine stump. As the figure in Dahlem reminds us to see and touch, we must pursue the wonders of nature when it may not be comfortable for us.

225. Bark keeps things in that should stay in and keeps things out that should stay out.

226. Tree people have been known to fall out of their patient and suffer injuries.

227. I went looking for heartrot and found CODIT instead.

228. The Krebs cycle is not a type of motorbike.

229. Golgi bodies are not people from outer space.

230. Trees never lie.

231. Trees are the most giving and forgiving organisms on earth.

232. Beware of so-called tree experts who do not understand tree biology.

233. Training beyond intelligence is dangerous.

234. Why is a molecule reduced when it gains electrons?

235. Trees support more communities of organisms than any other organism on earth.

236. Some researchers would rather look for it than find it.

237. If the research involves hard or dirty work, it probably has not been done.

238. We know very little about life below frozen soils.

239. Engineers are straight lines. Biologists are circles. It is time to connect the two in our cities.

240. Common sense is an oxymoron.

18.   Mycorrhizae and root hairs are on this root. The mycorrhizae are ecto forms. The root was in non-frozen soils below frozen soils. Root hairs often grow on mycorrhizae. Root hairs are extensions of single epidermal cells.

241. Gravity pulls things downward. Evaporation pulls things upward. Greed pulls things apart.

242. Happiness is walking among trees during a snowfall.

243. There is nothing more sweet than the one jellybean you find in your pocket after you thought they were all gone.

244. Not fair! In a wood chopping contest Joe took ash and gave Bill elm. Joe understood anatomy.

245. Dutch elm disease gave America a wake up call about city trees.

246. Some people get pimples. Some trees get burls.

247. Some people believe that early humans swung from trees – early swingers.

248. Trees and their associates were the first conglomerate.

249. Trees were the endless enemy to the first colonists.

250. People who touch trees do care for the trees and the world we share.

251. If the tree did not die immediately, the treatment must have been successful.

252. Medical doctors take an oath not to cause harm. Tree people should take a similar oath for trees.

253. Every system will have its pathogens. Think about it.

254. Predisposition agents and conditions slowly destroy defense systems.

255. Cellulose is sugar for the fungi.

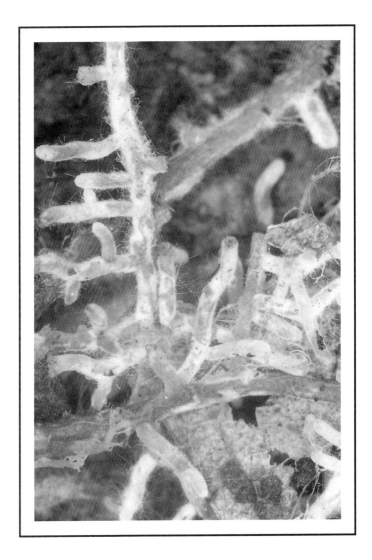

19. These mycorrhizae were between decaying leaves. I believe the fungi gain nutrients not only from the tree, but from dead leaves and wood. This is why composted leaves and wood as mulch is so very important for healthy trees.

256. Trees came with composted wood and leaves around their bases.

257. Because the tree top is dormant does not mean the roots are dormant.

258. Root hairs are extensions of single epidermal cells.

259. Fungi have chitin in their boundary walls.

260. Fungi absorb from the outside inward. Our guts absorb from the inside outward.

261. Chitin is a slightly altered form of cellulose. Chitin contains nitrogen.

262. Natural successions are highly ordered sequences of organisms that benefit the survival of the entire group.

263. If decay developed at will in trees, few infected trees would stand up.

264. Trees and people are about 98% by weight carbon, hydrogen, oxygen, nitrogen, sulfur, and phosphorus.

265. The four major compounds in all living things are carbohydrates, lipids, proteins, and nucleic acids.

266. Trees are mostly carbohydrates – cellulose. Humans are mostly proteins.

267. Natural systems come with many buffers. But, there are limits to those.

268. Sprouts form when fuel reserves get low.

269. Urea was made in the laboratory by Franz Whöler in 1828. This rocked the church.

20.   These mycorrhizae are smooth and not covered by
        hyphae. They may be a form more closely related to the
        endo types. Sometimes intermediate forms are called
        enectomycorrhizae because they seem to have some
        features of both ectos and endos. Note the many root
        hairs also on this root.

270. The sheep called Dolly was cloned in 1997. This also rocked the church and many governments.

271. Anatomy must precede physiology.

272. We have a name for people who see fast. We call them lucky!

273. There are two times when flying could be scary – take off and landing. There are two times when trees are vulnerable – leaf flush and leaf shedding.

274. What lives in a silver tube and eats peanuts? A frequent flyer!

275. To fire a gun it must be loaded, cocked, and trigger pulled. So it is with tree cracks, sun scald, and other problems.

276. It is better to have one fox in the chicken coop that eats a chicken now and then, than no foxes now and have a group of them come later and kill all of the chickens. Wetwood is the fox in a tree's chicken coop.

277. *Fomes pini* is the rabbit in the briar patch. The fungus thrives on the wood altered by the defense process.

278. There was a person who could hit golf balls 300 yards or more directly from tee off to the greens. The problem was his putts were the same way. The game is not over until the ball is in the hole.

279. A starving, tired lion in a cage can be killed by kitty cats. Predisposition.

280. Pathogens plug into your battery, and wallet.

281. *Helicobacter pylori*, not stress, causes ulcers. Once we know the cause, the cure is easy.

21. Mycorrhizae and root hairs are often called absorbing roots or non-woody roots because they have little lignin. The boundaries of root hairs are mostly cellulose while the boundaries of the hyphae are mostly chitin.

282.   Experience means avoiding the hits.

283.   When you ask nature the right question, you already have half of the answer.

284.   There are so many roads in our forests that you could never get lost.

285.   Die and kill are not the same. As trees die slowly, they increase the amount of exudates into the rhizosphere. When trees are killed suddenly and taken away, this does not happen.

286.   You can put a Rolls Royce engine in a small car, and soon other parts will fail.

287.   Walt Disney said you must first get people to say, "WOW", and then you go on to entertain them and to finally educate them.

288.   If your right foot goes down when the bass drum sounds, you will be in step with the drummer, but out of step with the music. I have seen an entire band in step with the drummer and out of step with the music. I see this in non-musical groups often.

289.   Consider the birds that walked to a flying workshop, learned to fly, and then walked home.

290.   The tree and fungus met at the bar. The tree said they had to pay ten dollars a kilo for phosphorus. The fungus said they had to pay ten dollars a kilo for carbohydrate. A deal was born. The fungus sold trees phosphorus for a dollar a kilo in exchange for the tree selling them carbohydrate for a dollar a kilo. This is the true story of how mycorrhizae and synergy started.

22. Woody roots on some tree species grow very deep as shown here on a pine from sandy soils in Texas.

291. Give a tree a shower. Cut away the dead branches.

292. Animal cells are like jelly bags. So long as your jelly bags jiggle, you are alive and well.

293. The good and bad things in life happen in periods of three minutes or less.

294. Define yourself with ten key words. If you cannot do it, you may have a problem.

295. Nature comes with bumps.

296. I found a skeleton in a tree cavity. He was the 1970 hide and seek champion.

297. The little boy pumping the organ reminded the player that WE will play Bach's Toccata and Fugue in G minor.

298. The chlorophyll molecule looks like a tree.

299. A tourniquet will stop a nosebleed! This is how I see injections and implants.

300. I wanted to publish a book without words. I could not come up with a title!

301. Glucose — magic springs, or soluble battery.

302. Dead stubs are sticks of sugar for the fungi.

303. Lignin is natural cement.

304. When lots of lignin came in trees, lots of dinosaurs left the earth.

305. Philosophy is a delightful mental trip around a circle.

23.   On other tree species, woody roots may be very shallow. The pine roots here were only a few centimeters below the soil surface. They were in sandy soil from Florida. Some woody roots grow shallow and far beyond the drip line of the tree. To learn about woody and non-woody roots, get a shovel and dig!

306. If you call north cold and south warm, you are not a worldly person.

307. Natural systems are not altruistic. Every member must pay dues, or else.

308. ATP is the living, international currency.

309. Why arsenic and old lace? Because arsenic is an analog for phosphorus. When arsenic bumps phosphorus in ATP, the cash flow stops. Death.

310. Nature cannot add. Four hydrogens of 1.008 weight each on the sun form helium of 4.0026. Was mass destroyed? $E = mc^2$ explains it all, and we get light and life as a result of the sun's fusion process. Learn about it!

311. Ammonium ion is the same as a wild red sports car. Nitrate ion is the same as an eighteen wheeler. When the sports car can break away from the eighteen wheeler, it moves rapidly. That is called an explosion.

312. Clays are party centers. They have lots of negative spots that attract the wandering positive ions. Fun!

313. A business that does not understand overhead and cash flow will surely fail.

314. There still is no free lunch. The second law will get you if you don't watch out.

315. Trees spend their money five ways: growth, maintenance, exudates, reproduction, and storage for defense.

316. Your workers are the symplast. The buildings and machines are the apoplast.

24. Woody roots support the tree, transport elements essential for life, store energy reserves, and synthesize substances essential for life. Some woody roots on tropical trees have anatomical features like stems above and like roots below.

317. You can have a full gas tank, but if your battery is dead, you will not start.

318. Trees store their money in the symplast. As the symplast decreases, so does storage space.

319. As storage of energy reserves decrease, so does the defense potential. Pathogens seem to know this very well.

320. My Christmas tree was cut in December. In April it was green and looked alive. But, it had a serious problem. Insects and fungi "seem to know" when the curve is only downward.

321. Two years after my house was painted, I saw a small unpainted spot where a ladder was put against the house. From that day on, and no matter how I passed the house, I saw the unpainted spot. Once you see something, it is difficult to not see it no matter how you look.

322. When growth, or mass, exceeds the amount of energy available to maintain order, the system will fail.

323. Anybody can take a clock apart. Some can put it back together. The real feat is to have it run again.

324. Is water good or bad? Too much will kill you and you will die when you don't get enough. Dose is the thing.

325. Arboriculture was founded on three treatments: flush cuts, paint, dig out cavities. All were injurious to trees.

326. A person once told me he cut the top off his tree so that it would not break off in a storm. If you cut your leg off, you will never have a broken ankle. Wow!

327. Many people kill trees with love; too much water and fertilizer.

25.   Roots are usually the first structures to emerge from a
       seed. Because roots depend on leaves for their energy, the
       leaves usually form after the energy reserves in the seed
       have been used to establish a root system.

328. Microorganisms have their picnics and parties under wound dressings.

329. It is the wound dressing idea more than the material that is dangerous.

330. Heartrot and wound dressings are twins.

331. When life is zigging and you are zagging, you will have a problem.

332. When proteins are tanned by phenols, the molecules look like a collapsed slinky toy. Once collapsed, enzymes cannot get in to break down the molecules.

333. The protection system of yaks that worked for them for millions of years worked against them when man and guns came. Yaks circle their young when threatened. They were easy targets for the pioneers. How many other long standing natural protection systems has man destroyed?

334. Galileo said his critics would not look through his telescope.

335. Kant said he was more disturbed by being misunderstood than criticized.

336. The cave shadow watchers described by Plato are still very active today.

337. The philosopher Berkeley said you must doubt first and then resolve your doubts to be a true believer.

338. A walnut veneer log buyer first called my attention to the defects caused by flush cuts.

339. People who work with trees every day know much more than they are able to explain.

26.   In propagating woody plants, many techniques are used to stimulate root growth. The magnolia here will grow from roots formed by a wounding procedure called air layering.

340. Termites that eat wood in living trees follow the CODIT patterns.

341. When you are too close to some wall paper designs, all looks disordered. When you go far back, the same disorder appears. When you find the best viewing distance, the repeats are seen, and they are orderly. Our perception of material order depends on our vantage point.

342. Pull a coiled spring outward and when you release it, it moves back to its original state. Pull the spring until the metal fatigues and when you release it, it will not return to its original position. First is stress, the second was strain.

343. Magicians convince you that the hat is empty. They start with a false premise.

344. To write a textbook, get five other textbooks and you cannot go wrong. Too often the same myths are repeated.

345. You should not write about things you have not done.

346. Humans have one mouth and two ears. There is a message there.

347. The body parts were arguing about who is the greatest. One part said it would shut down until the argument was settled. Soon they realized that all were equally important for the system to function properly. Connections.

348. Years ago we were told to put something hot on burns. Now we know something cold is better. We must accept adjustments that benefit us and others.

27.   Roots may cause some people problems. Maybe the trees
       are looking for "revenge" because the root problems
       usually occur as a result of confining a tree to a small
       space, as show here, or when trees are planted too deep.
       Then new roots form on some species, and as the roots
       grow upward they cause sidewalk cracks.

349. Athlete's foot is caused by bacteria. Later the fungi come. If you treat only the secondary agent, the problem will not go away. Treating secondary agents associated with tree problems is legion.

350. If a three micron long bacterium were enlarged to the size of a six-foot tall person, and then the person was enlarged the same way, the person would be about 700 miles tall. Yes, bacteria are small.

351. Sanitation was a major factor benefiting the health of humans.

352. What do you think are the ten most important events (religious events aside) that shaped the progress of humans?

353. The cambial zone is the same as the queen bee. Both must be fed by others and their job is to pump out new living cells.

354. Some predators are not very patient. They want to kill something, now.

355. The Little Fox said you become responsible forever for whatever you tame (Antoine de Saint Exupery, The Little Prince). We tamed our city trees.

356. Leonardo da Vinci said to paint the outside of a body he must first understand the inside. Human anatomy was born. Vesalius also dissected many bodies.

357. Alexander Fleming was guilty of a poor practice done by many mycologists. They leave the culture plates around too long. Fleming was able to see things. From his work came penicillin, the wonder antibiotic of all time.

28.   Planting too deep is a common mistake. Some trees form surface roots that may circle the base or the surface roots disrupt lawns.

358. Antibiotics are mimics. The key goes in but it will not turn, and you cannot insert another key.

359. Around 1845 the germ theory began to be accepted. This was the most turbulent time in science.

360. School children in France recently named Louis Pasteur as the most famous Frenchman of all times.

361. When Pasteur was doing his work, the establishment did not consider him a hero. The same with Leonardo da Vinci.

362. Almost a century before Pasteur, Spallanzani in Italy said the same things, and again the ruling establishment of scientists (?) cut him down.

363. It is sad but true when you consider that the people who made some of the most important discoveries of all times were hated by their contemporaries.

364. Mendel had to watch his papers burn.

365. Galileo had to crawl on his belly and say he was wrong.

366. Carl Sagan and Jacques Cousteau were not considered real scientists by most of the establishment. How sad!

367. Meristematic points form spear-like points into the bark. The points can differentiate to form sprouts, flowers, or roots. Other types of spear-like points go from the bark into the wood. These are associated with a wood pattern called bird's eye. The initiating factors must come from the bark.

368. Read the history of science by George Sarton.

29.　In the beginning, grass and trees grew in their own territories. Now people want them to grow together. When grass is overwatered, as shown here, tree roots suffer and death is common. This poor magnolia is well on the way. Sad!

369. Meristematic means the capacity to form new cells that differentiate to form new tissues or organs.

370. Meristems are cells that have the ability to form new cells that can differentiate to form new tissues or organs. The action of meristems is under genetic control, and other factors may stimulate their start up.

371. Trees grow as the meristems form cells that differentiate to be all the tissues and organs in a tree.

372. Einstein said explanations should be as simple as possible, but no simpler.

373. Sir Francis Bacon tried to preserve chickens by filling their bodies with snow. In the process he got so cold that he soon died.

374. The black plague was one of the worst catastrophes ever inflicted on humans. A little sanitation would have saved most of the people.

375. Make a horse thirsty. You could then put the water anywhere and it will be found.

376. The researcher took all the legs off a flea. He then shouted to the flea to jump. The flea just lay there. The report stated that fleas lose their ability to hear when you remove their legs. Don't laugh. I have seen research reports worse than that.

377. Mature people complete things.

378. All systems have an Achilles' heel.

379. I have never learned how not to feel pain when hurt. I have learned to shorten the hurt period by getting up and going again after a hit.

30. The grass, tree problem is not only a city one; it is common in parks and forests as the sides of roads are seeded. The live oaks in this California park are ready to give up after trying to live with the grass for many years.

380. You know you are on to something hot when it makes your critics steam.

381. The playing field defines the game. A hockey puck on a basketball court is just as bad as a basketball on a hockey ice rink.

382. Root hairs often grow on mycorrhizae.

383. Recognition never exceeds criticism.

384. If you don't show slides, they want their money back.

385. I would like to see a meeting where at least half of the time the lights were on.

386. When ten heads bob within one minute, it is time for a break, regardless of what the program says.

387. What are forest ecosystems? Forests are ecosystems!

388. Hydrogen bonds are similar to post-it notes. They stick when you want them to stick, and when you unstick them you cannot tell where they were stuck.

389. Serendipity works best the faster you move.

390. After the race is over, your speed means nothing.

391. Would you let a person who calls himself a car mechanic open your hood if he did not know what a spark plug was? How about a tree expert and the symplast?

392. Successions of microorganisms lead to tooth decay.

393. Tooth decay is the most common human disease.

394. Words understood by the mind lead the hand in actions.

31.　Woody roots are storage organs. As energy storage is depleted, opportunistic pathogens attack. Most root diseases start when root defense, which is based on energy storage, is low. To show energy storage, a stain containing iodine can be poured over a freshly cut surface. The maple root at left is dark purple indicating an abundance of energy reserves in the form of starch. The specimen at right is from the trunk of the same tree. The living cells in the trunk do store starch, but not as much as the roots do.

395. There is mounting scientific evidence that Humpty-Dumpty was pushed!

396. Wet spaghetti bends. So long as wetwood lubricates branch cracks, the branches bend. When the wetwood fluids dry, the branch could break.

397. Nature abhors virulence. Too few get too much.

398. There is almost no waste in natural systems.

399. All organisms die three major ways: depletion of fuel, dysfunction of parts and processes, and disruption as by sudden hit or storms.

400. Olive trees have been beat on more than any other tree. In tree heaven the *Ficus benjamina* will get the second place for human abuses.

401. Many people will buy anything they believe will correct their mistakes or cover up their ignorance.

402. George Bernard Shaw said he became recognized because he was able to think for ten minutes each day.

403. Soil redox reaction and soccer are similar; no intermissions.

404. I wish I could find the book of "They". "They" say this. "They" say that, etc.

405. According to the laws of aerodynamics, bumble bees cannot fly.

406. Airplanes are most efficient just before they run out of fuel.

32.   Here are actinorhizae on non-woody roots on alder. Actinorhizae are organs that are made up of tree and actinomycete tissues. Actinomycetes are microorganisms that have some features similar to bacteria and fungi. The actinorhizae fix atmospheric pure nitrogen to ammonia, which can be chemically altered by some bacteria to nitrate ions.

407. Storks were compacting the soil in the grain fields. The grand committee said a person should chase away the storks. Then a greater problem was started by compaction due to the stork chaser. The grand committee then said to eliminate compaction by the stork chaser, he should be carried on a platform by four people. The grand committee was hailed for their intelligence in preventing compaction by the storks and the stork chaser who now rode on a platform. No comment on the rest of this story.

408. A farmer had a single mule with extra large eye shields pulling the plow. He called out to the mule by at least six different names. A city person watched this for a while and finally asked the farmer why does he call the mule by six different names. The farmer said if the mule knew he was the only one pulling the plow he would stop. The city person went back and invented the committee.

409. Be careful who you show your big red balloon. Some people delight in putting pins in them.

410. When you see a naked king, you do not need an experiment to prove he has no clothes on.

411. Faith, Fear and Fun are the three major motivators in life.

412. Try to touch a spider web without causing it to jiggle.

413. Just because you have a green light does not mean you should proceed when a large truck is going through the red light.

414. Why are they usually referred to as red lights and not traffic lights?

415. Common sense is constructive philosophy.

416. First aid, then cosmetics.

33.   Lichens are organisms made up of fungi and algae connected in highly ordered ways that ensure benefits to both organisms.

As they grow and respire they give off carbon dioxide and water. As some of the carbon dioxide dissolves in water, carbonic acid forms. The acid decomposes rocks very slowly and essential elements are released for growth of trees and many other organisms. They do not injure trees.

417. Smiles start endorphins.

418. There once was a person who knew it all. He went to a meeting and stayed in the hall. He did not know why, his friends passed him by. What was there to talk about after all?!

419. You can communicate with nature if you understand the language.

420. You cannot communicate with anything or anybody when it is in a survival mode.

421. Learning starts when you doubt something. Learning happens when you resolve your doubts.

422. People who knowingly plant tall-maturing trees under utility lines should be punished.

423. There is no discussion with a person who has a closed mind.

424. A professional is a person who understands dose.

425. A code of ethics is the foundation of a profession.

426. Remember, it could be worse.

427. Comfort rarely leads to progress.

428. Few things of importance ever happened without controversy first.

429. It is not what you make, but what you keep that is important.

430. Read. Read. Read.

431. There is no such thing as a cruise in life.

34.   When possible, grow trees in groups or clusters. These
       live oaks in Texas appear as one beautiful tree.

432. Researchers, show me your data, then let us talk.

433. If a bacterium multiplied under optimum conditions for three days, its mass would be greater than that of the earth.

434. As humans kill more big things, many more little things are there to take over.

435. You can't kill viruses by building a bigger sledgehammer.

436. When climbers fall down, workmen's compensation goes up.

437. There is no such thing as "green waste." It should be called natural recyclables.

438. There are three major ways to stimulate a person: pain, pleasure, curiosity.

439. When electrons shift position, oxidation-reduction processes go on. When protons shift positions, acid-base reactions go on.

440. If you have to keep telling people how great you are, maybe you're not.

441. I have always had the greatest respect for people who work hard with trees.

442. You can show 80 slides in one minute. Try it.

443. Being busy does not mean the same thing as being productive.

444. People who think they are sophisticated usually are.

445. The Sophists were masters of rhetoric.

35. Trees and their associates benefit greatly from decomposed leaves and wood. The material supplies an energy source and elements that are essential for a healthy life. Steve Nimz in Hawaii shows mulch from leaves and wood after six months of composting. This material is food for the tree system.

446. Naked kings seem to be on the increase.

447. Scientists are fast.

448. Having lots of trees is different from having lots of high quality trees.

449. Trying to treat what you do not understand is the same as trying to start a Rolls Royce by hitting it with a sledgehammer.

450. If you can't explain to your family what you are doing, you have a problem.

451. Isoprene is the basic molecule of natural rubber.

452. Phenols are the basic molecules in angiosperms that polymerize to form protection substances.

453. Free radicals are not protesting people.

454. Stay reduced! Don't rust!

455. Only a very few graduates from a very prestigious U.S. university in 1996 knew why the earth has seasons.

456. Aim for targets, not shadows.

457. If you want to know how many teeth in a horse's mouth, you find a friendly horse and count.

458. Airports are bleak places. Consider some of their words: terminal, departure, last call, final destination.

459. To test the translation features of a computer, an English message was translated to Russian and then back to English. The message was, "The spirit is willing but the flesh is weak." It came back as, "The whiskey is cheap but the meat is rotten."

36. In Victoria, British Columbia, Canada, mulch piles of leaves and wood chips are kept cooler by perforated plastic pipes. The composted material is the best material to spread about the base of trees. The mulch should be no more than five to ten centimeters thick. Avoid piling mulch against the base of trees.

460. What you say and what people hear can be very different. (And scary if you are a speaker!)

461. People often hear only what they want to hear.

462. Many people are not hard-of-hearing but hard-of-listening.

463. Oxygen is nice but greedy – electronegative.

464. Hydrogen is fickle – always changing position.

465. Nitrogen is a mover – it wants to get back to the air.

466. Carbon is friendly – the mother element of life.

467. Bacterial erosion of the pits in spruce is the secret of Stradivarius violins.

468. Conifers have tracheids with pits.

469. Pits regulate flow of liquids. Pits are made up of a central torus and a webwork structure called the margo.

470. Gymnosperms have naked seeds. Angiosperms have covered seeds.

471. Monocots have one seedleaf. Dicots have two seedleaves.

472. The symplast stores energy reserves. The apoplast stores bound water.

473. Bound water is water bonded to the hydroxyls on cellulose by hydrogen bonds.

474. Free water flows, bound water does not.

475. Many soil insects and mycorrhizae do not freeze. They supercool.

37.　In the research park in Hawaii, the trees are mulched with composted leaves and wood chips to reduce mowing, prevent picnic soil compaction, to reduce potential accidents due to people under trees, and to promote healthy growth, and to save money.

476. I know mycorrhizae are active in non-frozen soils beneath frozen soils in winter.

477. Soils are alive with many organisms in winter. (Remember, the best fishing places in the world are in cold water.)

478. Trunk cortex is green and can photosynthesize when conditions are proper, even when leaves are gone.

479. Some trees move oxygen into roots through a special tissue called aerenchyma in the cortex.

480. For people who think wood anatomy and tree anatomy are the same, I would like to see them put their fork into a steak that is still on the hoof.

481. Insects keep nitrogen high in the soil.

482. The Everglades were seeded with *Melaleuca*.

483. Chemical pathways have shunts. Roads have detours.

484. Suberin is made up of long branched chains of fatty acids.

485. Acids are proton donors. Bases are proton acceptors.

486. Water can act as an acid or base in chemical reactions.

487. I know a person who said he could save any tree – along the driveway, in the barn, stacked next to the house, etc.

488. Green begats green. Where there is money, there are trees.

489. Synergy is two people making a king-sized bed.

490. When they said I could look at their black walnut trees, they did not know I meant on the inside.

38.　This coastal redwood in central California is very healthy mainly because of the mulch of composted redwood needles and wood chips. The grass appears greener at the boundary of the brown mulch. Bark mulch does not break down to release elements essential for life.

491. My biology professor once asked his professor before a test whether he wanted the correct answers or the ones he gave them.

492. A lion in a cage and a lion in the field are two different things.

493. In metabolism, ions play bumper cars.

494. Root exudates are like taxes.

495. Master the small words, and gain the large audience.

496. Real power is having, but not using, the power to kill.

497. *Cola nitida* produces flavoring and cocaine.

498. If you think all chemicals are bad, don't drink water or eat food.

499. A hundred million carbon atoms in a line would measure about three centimeters.

500. Carbon dioxide in water forms some carbonic acid.

501. The pale blue color of ice is due to hydrogen bonding of water.

502. Consider poor Joe who liked alcohol. Drank methanol rather than ethanol. He then quickly learned, as his brain got burned. That words are important after all.

503. Cacao beans that produce chocolate are white. Why do we make white chocolate brown and brown vanilla white?

504. You know you're a Depression Era Kid if you remember squeezing the yellow dye into white margarine.

39.   Young trees and young children require special attention. Children are born with a strong curiosity for natural things. We must encourage this curiosity, not dull or destroy it.

505. Soaps are the original double agents. One end is soluble in oils and the other is soluble in water.

506. Leaves are all colors except green. That's why they appear green. Think about it.

507. Joseph Priestly called it rubber because it could erase pencil marks.

508. Natural rubber comes from *Hevea brasiliensis* and from dandelions, *Taraxacum officinale*.

509. Glucose is usually in the form of a ring.

510. Dextrose is glucose that rotates polarized light to the right.

511. Glucose is the fuel of life.

512. Fructose is also known as levulose because it rotates polarized light to the left. It also tastes sweeter to us.

513. Our stomach cannot digest some complex sugars, such as those found in beans. The sugars go to the large intestines where the bacterium *Escherichia coli* does break them down and in the process forms the gases hydrogen, carbon dioxide and methane. Now you know!

514. *Escherichia coli* is very beneficial to us so long as it stays in its place.

515. Starch is the major energy storage material of trees.

516. Starch is not soluble in water.

517. Cellulose is the most abundant natural substance in the world.

40.   Children enjoy planting trees. We must make certain that
        they are taught correct practices at the beginning.

518. The only sure way to know if a wild mushroom is poisonous is to have one person eat it and a second person follow him for a few days.

519. Many people failed biology because they misspelled photosynthesis and chlorophyll.

520. Some tree people top trees in revenge of their biology teachers.

521. In the beginning we know now what was done. Woman and man were meant to be one. To care for the garden, the environment and trees. To dress it and to keep it for you and for me.

522. What is your salt index? Do you: See or just look? Act or just wait? Listen or just hear? Touch or just watch?

523. I believe the real constant is the amount of protoplasm on earth. When someone loses weight, another person gains it.

524. A gametophyte is not a brawl.

525. Euthanasia is not children in the Orient.

526. Rocks are nature's slow release fertilizers.

527. Life's amino acids are mostly left handed.

528. The alien reported that earthlings spend most of their time hitting balls. Think how many ball-hitting games we have.

529. Life is run by a little power from the sun.

530. Education is a process not a product.

531. If you can't laugh at yourself, others will.

41.   Young trees and young children suffer when incorrect treatments and information are given. Wounding at planting time set the stage for serious decay. Incorrect information inflicted on children also leads to future problems as curiosity begins to decay and biology becomes the enemy.

532. "Sustainable" has taken over "hopefully" as the most used buzz word.

533. People who think all fungi are bad should go without wine, cheese and bread for starters.

534. Trunk wrap on young trees prevents the green cortex from photosynthesizing.

535. There are no data to show that trunk wraps prevent "frost" cracks or sun scald.

536. Contact parenchyma connect axial and radial parenchyma.

537. Paraformaldehyde pills used by the maple tapping people kill contact parenchyma. Vessel plugging is stalled and sap flows longer. Decay-causing fungi love it! I hear that many over-tapped and pill-treated trees die from acid rain.

538. You are what you eat. Minute amounts of microelements can cause big changes in the ways fungi grow.

539. We are made up of many little things that, taken separately, are not so important. But, when they are all connected, they become you, and that is important. The same with trees.

540. Decay is a process where highly ordered substances become disordered. As order goes to disorder, energy is released. As disorder goes to order, energy is consumed.

541. Decay is a process. Decayed wood is the product of the process. Decaying is the kinetic state of the process.

542. Wounds are mechanical disruptions that alter the high order of an organism, thus causing injury.

42.   Pity this young tree! It is tied tightly at four positions. The guard at the base has been cut by a string trimmer that also wounded the trunk. The string trimmer came because grass was wanted about the tree base. The light ensures that you see this torture at night also. Sad! When will we ever learn?

543. Injury is a physiological disruption, and damage is an economic disruption.

544. Cambium miner tracks in paper birch cause very little injury to the tree but a great amount of damage to the veneer.

545. Some diseases cause serious injury to trees, but the trunks can be salvaged for high quality products, and little damage results.

546. Socrates said, "Know the man by the words he uses."

547. Apoptosis is programmed cell death. In animals, the dead cells are lysed – broken down – and new cells are formed in the same places. In trees, the dead cells stay in place and act as storage places for bound water and for structural support.

548. Maybe life is the highest order of light? Think of all the references to light. "I am the light of the world." "Out of darkness came light." "They left the darkness of the cave and went out into the world of light." Etc.

549. Light is both a particle, a photon, and a wave. This is an example of a duality. The world of natural systems is full of dualities, and even some trialities.

550. Trees pay taxes in the form of root exudates. Percentages of photosynthate, and other substances made that can leave the roots as exudates range from 5% to 40%. As trees decline, the percentage increases.

43.   As trees grow older, the torture continues as they are not
        only braced in ways that prevent swaying but wrapped
        with various materials. The materials prevent
        photosynthesis in the young green cortex. There are no
        data to show that wrapping prevents problems.

551. The self-thinning rule of ecology states that on a given site, as some trees increase in mass, the number of trees on the site decreases. As some of the trees die, their exudates increase and benefit soil microorganisms. This process has high survival value in a forest, but may not be effective in cities where individual trees are removed as they die.

552. Give freely of your ideas and you will never die.

553. Natural laws are almost right most of the time.

554. To learn you must first teach.

555. Survival depends on rate of recognition, decision making, and adjustments. A feedback process.

556. <u>Wood is dead</u> and <u>decay is not a disease</u> are the two myths that have caused, and still are causing, confusion with tree biology and tree care.

557. Would you buy and use a product that gave you perfect teeth, but rotted your gums? We must care for the soils.

558. Wood cells are arranged in ways that support the tree as a biological and mechanical system.

559. All wood cells are born alive.

560. There are three basic types of wood cells: transport cells – vessels, tracheids – mechanical support cells – fibers, fiber tracheids —, and cells that contain living substances for a few to many years – parenchyma, axial and radial.

561. Conifer wood is made up mostly of tracheids and fiber tracheids, from a volume basis.

562. On a number-of-cell basis, sapwood contains more living cells than dead cells. The living cells make up the symplast.

44.   The wire-in-the-hose torture continues. When trees require bracing, elastic materials should be used that do not injure the bark. The tree should be braced as low as possible on the trunk to allow swaying.

563. Diffuse-porous wood has vessels, parenchyma, and fibers of about the same size arranged equally throughout the entire growth increment.

564. Ring-porous wood has large diameter vessels in the beginning of the growth increment, and the vessels decrease in diameter as the growth increment develops.

565. Vessels do end. Vessels begin as single living cells that join at their top and bottom to form a short conduit. Other vessel conduits connect from the sides to form a transport pathway from root tips to leaf tips.

566. There are limits to every system.

567. Every organism must rest.

568. If ants in their present form grew to the size of elephants, their bodies would be crushed by gravity.

569. System mechanics is a fancy way to say the way things work.

570. Reading gets your engines going.

571. Computers are great, but they will never replace touching the real thing.

572. Microorganisms alter wood six basic ways: white rot, brown rot, discolored wood, wetwood, soft rot, and pit erosion.

573. White rot – cellulose and lignin digested. Brown rot – cellulose digested, lignin altered. Discolored wood – cell contents and walls altered, color change. Wetwood – cell contents and walls altered by anaerobes mostly, not always a color change. Soft rot – cell walls eroded with distinct patterns. Pit erosion – pits selectively digested, mostly in ponded logs.

45.   Problems start when defective trees leave the nursery, such as this London Plane that was just planted. Dr. Daniele Zanzi points to the crack and four stems. This poor tree will not last long. We must buy only healthy trees free of defects, and develop strong specifications for what is acceptable.

574. Fibers have thick cell walls. The secondary wall is divided into an S_1, S_2, and S_3 layer. The S_2 layer in the middle is the thickest.

575. The S_2 layer is the major site for bound water.

576. Fiber saturation point means the saturation of the cell walls with water, but not the cell lumen. The f.s.p. – fiber saturation point – of cell walls ranges from 25 to 35% moisture.

577. Moisture content of wood is measured as the percentage of water weight to wood weight when volume remains constant. Most living trees have moisture contents of about 80% and above. A 100% moisture content means the weight of water and the weight of oven-dried wood in a block of wood are equal. It is possible to have moisture contents far above 100% in living trees.

578. Water is the only substance on earth that normally exists in three forms: solid ice, gas and a liquid.

579. Water is made up of one oxygen atom and two hydrogen atoms. The way the connections are made is one of the wonders of this world.

580. Water molecules "stick" to other water molecules because of hydrogen bonds. This cohesive characteristic of water makes it possible for it to be held within the transport stream.

581. A retired fighter pilot said, "Real stress is seeing your name on the roster for a mission that has had a 50% no return record."

582. Forests can heal, trees cannot.

46.   John Martin points to a later stage of the defect shown in
        the previous photo. This tree was planted four years
        before the photo was taken. The growing stems have
        squeezed the cambium to death. Wetwood fluids are
        flowing from the injured tissues. What must be done to
        stop this?

583. You can feed the tree system, but not trees.

584. Composted wood and leaves are tree system food.

585. Rather than spending time and effort trying to find better ways to cut a shrinking pie, spend the time and effort on getting a larger pie.

586. From the first propeller planes to the modern jets, the principles of flying have changed very little.

587. When a tree is wounded, you should not treat only the wound but the entire tree.

588. Trees wound themselves as stems grow together. Cracks often follow. The same events occur with roots and cracks that develop upward on the trunk.

589. Just as branches die and leave stubs that are openings into the trunk, roots also die and leave root stubs. Microorganisms do not have to "look hard" for ways to get into trees.

590. Longevity of trees is strongly related to the resisting force of the protection zone that forms at the branch base after the branch dies.

591. Long living trees, such as white oaks and redwoods, have strong branch protection zones. Gray birch and cherry have very weak branch protection zones.

592. As trees compartmentalize infected wood, storage space for energy reserves is reduced. Strong compartmentalization "keeps" the lost space to a minimum.

593. In physics it is called friction, and in business it is called overhead.

47.   The crimes against nature go on. This oak was planted
       directly under utility lines three years before the photo
       was taken. The only answer here is to post a heavy fine
       against anyone who plants a tall-maturing tree directly
       under a utility line. It would be great if our tree
       organizations would support such an action. I have tried.

594. The difficulty with generating systems is that as mass increases, the energy to maintain order in the mass increases at exponential rates.

595. The difficulty with regenerating systems is that as parts are constantly being replaced, wear begins to take its toll.

596. Natural systems will survive so long as they have enough time to adjust. When disruptions occur faster in time than the time required for adjustments, the system will begin to decline.

597. Reproduction takes a great amount of reserve energy.

598. No machine can start itself.

599. Inductive means to start at the beginning and move forward. Deductive means to start at the end and move backwards.

600. Phenology is the timing of natural processes: flushing, reproduction, wood formation, energy storage, shedding, dormancy.

601. Professionals keep records.

602. A very successful person told me that if you want to become successful, talk to someone you think is successful. I thought about it. Then I talked with a tree.

603. Clays are like sandwiches. Some are two layered and some are three layered.

604. Clays are crystals of aluminum, silicon, and oxygen mostly.

48.   In some cities, such as St. Paul, Minnesota shown here, young trees are being trained to grow away from utility lines

605.	Some clays, especially the two layered clays, increase or decrease their charges as pH increases or decreases. Two to one clays or the three layered clays have a permanent charge not affected by pH.

606.	A pH of 7 means that 0.0000001 moles of active hydrogen protons are in solution.

607.	A mole is a gram equivalent weight of an element in a liter of water. For example, hydrogen has a molecular weight of one, so a mole of hydrogen is one gram of hydrogen per liter. Oxygen weighs 16 on the molecular scale, so 16 grams of oxygen in one liter of water is one mole of oxygen.

608.	Before elements can be absorbed by roots, they must be in the form of ions that are soluble in water. This is good news and bad news because soluble ions can also be leached from the soil.

609.	When nitrogen as nitrate ion, NO_3^-, or as ammonium ion, NH_4^+, enter a non-woody root, the first thing the nitrogen does is to bond with carbon from reserves to form amino acids.

610.	Amino acids have a central carbon that has connected to it an NH_2 group, a hydrogen, a chain or ring of carbon groups, and a COOH group. The COOH, or carboxyl group, makes it an acid.

611.	One of the greatest pleasures of life is knowing just a little bit about the way things work.

612.	Leaves begin to die and then the abscission layer forms. Non-woody roots die after the abscission layer forms.

49. For older trees near utility lines, the 90-3-90 guide can be used. It states that 90 percent of the time, the removal of three branches will give 90 percent of the clearance.

613.   Cankers are localized dead spots. Lesions are dead spots that could spread. When lesions are localized, then they are called cankers.

614.   Most canker-causing microorganisms are opportunists that wait for the host's defense system to decrease.

615.   As bark turgor decreases, the likelihood of infection by a canker-causing organism increases.

616.   Angiosperms have phenol-based substances mostly as protection compounds. Gymnosperms have isoprene or terpene-based substances mostly as their protection compounds.

617.   Insects infest. Microorganisms infect.

618.   When flush pruning was considered correct, timing of pruning was extremely important because the cuts caused serious trunk injuries that removed the branch protection zone. When collar cuts are made, timing is not so important. Small mistakes that injure the collar or trunk during leaf flushing and leaf shedding can still cause injuries.

619.   Why is it that I am asked repeatedly to give new stuff while almost all the questions I get are the same old stuff?

620.   Growth is an increase in mass.

621.   Phytochromes form when light duration and intensity reach a certain level. The phytochromes "wake up" enzymes that release stored energy in starch, and start the machinery of life going.

622.   Askenasy was a Russian fruit horticulturist who worked out the phenological periods for apples and cherries.

50.   This American elm was pruned correctly to provide
       clearance. Directional pruning is different from 90-3-90.
       Too often in directional pruning, branches growing
       toward the lines are tipped. In 90-3-90 the entire branch
       growing toward the line should be removed.

623.   Load and unload are good descriptive terms that help to explain forces going inward, loading – and forces moving outward, unloading.

624.   Source is a term meaning the position of origin of a substance. Sink is the position where the substance finally is used or incorporated and cannot move further.

625.   Physics is the science of measuring forces.

626.   Pain is a stimulus that triggers movement away from a threatening agent or condition. Trees cannot move away and pain had no survival value.

627.   Boredom is a major cause of accidents. Robotic people get bored easily. Thinking people seldom get bored.

628.   Loving your work is different from understanding it. Both are necessary.

629.   Take some young people on a nature walk.

630.   As information increases, the need to know more details also increases.

631.   The theory of spontaneous generation stated that life just happened. As materials broke down, clusters of substances called monads formed microorganisms. The germ theory stated that microbes cause the breakdown of the substances.

632.   Before Robert Hartig, people believed that decay caused fungi. Hartig showed that fungi caused decay. The simple reversal of words set the stage for the science of forest pathology.

51. Some people believe that all trees should be cut because they drop leaves on the lawn and cause other equally "serious" problems for humans. Other extremists believe that no trees should be cut. Trying to find middle ground is not easy. We often forget that we humans are not alone on this planet and many other living things depend on trees for their lives.

633. The Mississippi Valley Laboratory in St. Louis was established in 1899. Dr. Herman von Schrenk was the director. Studies on wood decay and discoloration were done mostly. In time, the studies drifted toward wood products. In 1907 the lab was discontinued and the Forest Products Laboratory at Madison, Wisconsin took over. The major focus of the lab was on wood products decay. Tree biology never had a chance.

634. The six molecules that dominate life are glucose, water, carbon dioxide, oxygen, ammonia, and carbonic acid. Every "green" person should know something about them.

635. Have you ever thought what holds together all the atoms in your body or in a tree? Mostly small forces called hydrogen bonds.

636. If living things were not put together with weak forces, living things would never break down and new life would not have a chance.

637. When in doubt about a treatment, go slowly and lightly.

638. When Sputnik went off in October, 1957, science in America also went off. In the 1980's Sputnik crashed. No new science wave has started again.

639. Never in the history of humankind have so many people talked and written so much about what they know so little about – the environment.

640. I'm sure Mother Nature cries when she sees plastic bags full of leaves going to the dump.

641. Think of a world where all the "bad pathogens" went away.

52.   Many insects, fungi, bacteria, and other organisms are thought to be harmful, yet very few of them are. It is a pity when we use treatments that are designed to kill everything. So along with the few "bad guys" go all the "good guys." Then we want to buy the "good guys" and put them back. The insects and microorganisms have a job to do on earth. Many are "clean up" experts such as the fungus parasitizing the mushroom fruiting body of another fungus. These organisms break down dead organisms to release or recycle elements essential for new life. Some organisms attack others that no longer have a defense system. A few attack living organisms that are healthy.

642. Think for a moment of all the words we have to describe wood: sap, heart, wet, early, late, discolored, black, green, red, rose, soft, hard, spring, summer, dotty, fat, lighter, tension, compression, pulp, burl, root, trunk, branch, petrified, blue-stained, false heart, wound, round, violin, instrument, ring-porous, diffuse-porous, juvenile, sandal, ripe, tallow, brashy, composite, and the list probably goes on.

643. Optimization means the strength is highest at the point where most of the loading will take place.

644. As trees sway, reaction wood forms in places that optimize the strength of the trunk and branches.

645. Don't call a tree a hazard until it is one.

646. If a tree is weak structurally, but does not pose a hazard because of a lack of target, remember wildlife use such trees for shelter, nesting, and roosting.

647. Autopsy really means to see for yourself. Necropsy means dissection of the dead.

648. The more you can tell about a fallen tree from an autopsy, the more others will listen to you.

649. In legal matters your credentials are the most important part of the process.

650. The rhizosphere is the zone about one millimeter about the surface of absorbing non-woody roots, mycorrhizae, and the hyphae growing from the mycorrhizae.

651. The rhizoplane is the boundary between the tree tissues and the soil. Under the electron microscope it is difficult to tell the tree side from the soil side.

53. This beetle came from declining Monterey pines in California. Note that the body spines are well adapted for carrying spores of fungi from place to place.

652. The rhizoplane is the site of exudates.

653. For an anion to move into a non-wood root, an anion must exude from the root. The most common anion going in is nitrate and the most common anion going out is bicarbonate, and to a lesser amount, hydroxyl.

654. Respiration in roots produces carbon dioxide and water. Carbon dioxide in water forms some carbonic acid. Carbonic acid dissociates to form a hydrogen proton and hydrogen carbonate or bicarbonate anion.

655. Without oxygen, normal respiration does not take place.

656. Ammonium cation has a single positive charge. If clay is around, the cation usually bonds with the negative sites on the crystals.

657. The redox potential is a relative measure of electron activity in soils as oxidation and reduction take place.

658. In waterlogged soils where oxygen is low or lacking, iron and manganese become the electron acceptors. This leads to the precipitation of iron and manganese and the tree does not get any of these elements.

659. Humic and fulvic acids buffer pH swings in the soil.

660. People who call wonderful soil dirt need help.

661. People who try to play games with Mother Nature invariably lose in the end.

662. When you think humans have mastered this earth, consider earthquakes, floods, and hurricanes for starters.

663. Ectomycorrhizal fungi often are the major inhabitants of conifer forest soils.

54.   Other insects, such as this just-hatched gypsy moth larva, eat healthy leaves on several tree species. Repeated attacks year after year can so weaken some trees that other organisms attack and cause death. Note the spines that facilitate gliding on the wind over long distances.

664. About 95% or more of the nitrogen and sulfur is in an organic form in most surface soils.

665. Shedding of non-woody roots adds a great amount of carbon to soils.

666. Humic acids slow decomposition reactions in soils.

667. Hyphae from mycorrhizae on one tree can connect with hyphae from mycorrhizae from another tree of a different species. The grand forest connection.

668. Bacteria often live in tunnels left behind as hyphae of soil fungi die.

669. Amoebae are not able to attack the bacteria in the minute-diameter tunnels.

670. Soil actinomycetes are very tolerant of water stress. Actinomycetes often give that "good earth" aroma after a rain.

671. Carbon dioxide is more soluble in cold water.

672. Reduction and oxidation are molecular ping-pong.

673. Don't tell me what you are going to do, tell me what you have done.

674. Don't argue with anyone who is holding a running chainsaw.

675. Autotrophs make their own food. Heterotrophs have to have it made for them.

676. Bacteria have no membrane-bound nucleus.

55.   The clusters of mushrooms at the base of this ash indicate
      advanced decay. Many decay-causing fungi produce their
      spores on gills of mushrooms. Mushrooms are also the
      reproductive bodies of many beneficial fungi that form
      ectomycorrhizae.

677.   Many of the tree species that do well in cities got their genetic codes while growing in wet soils: ash, plane trees, red maples.

678.   Many species of *Ficus* are stranglers.

679.   Earthworms neutralize soil acidity.

680.   Blue-green algae are really cyanobacteria.

681.   A small fern in the genus *Azolla* lives in rice fields. Nodule-forming bacteria on the ferns fix nitrogen. Nitrogen fixation can also go on inside sugar cane.

682.   You cannot inoculate soils with mycorrhizae. Mycorrhizae are organs made up of tree and fungus tissues. You can inoculate soils with the fungi that infect roots to form mycorrhizae.

683.   Infection is a connecting process where substances move between two organisms of different species.

684.   Infections can be mutualistic, synergetic, or pathogenic.

685.   Pathogenesis is an infection process that benefits one organism – pathogen – to the detriment of the other – host.

686.   Disease is an abnormal physiological process that causes injury or death.

687.   Disease must be based on the entire organism and not just its parts.

688.   Inside the meeting halls many new things are discussed. Outside, the same old problems persist.

689.   The most difficult thing to change is an attitude.

56. Trees with extensive hollows are at high risk for fracture during moderate to high winds. This was fractured during near-hurricane force winds. Other trees without hollows also fractured during this storm. Cracks usually are more prone to fracturing than hollows.

690. While a child is sitting in front a television, give him or her some magnets to play with. Which gets the attention, the magnet or the TV, will tell you much about the child's future.

691. Touching means connecting. Learning biology is a touching situation.

692. Long-term studies and measurements in biology are sorely lacking.

693. The myth that trees are a renewable resource still persists.

694. Trying to grow trees in sick soils is the same as telling a person you have beautiful teeth but your gums must go.

695. Did you know there is a big push now to try to replace wood framing in houses with steel framing? Think of the consequences this will have, if it happens, on the forest industries.

696. I'm going to put a swing on that branch as soon as it grows a little higher as the tree ages! (Don't laugh, this is a more common belief than you think.)

697. The wound dressing myth will never die. The sad thing is that the myth is being taught by people who are supposed to be scientists.

698. Every child should have the opportunity to climb a tree.

699. How will we ever get to the excitement of electromagnetic fields when the same old stuff is still being taught: heartrot, wound dressings, plant food, and all types of cure-alls?

700. If all the magic wonderful cure-alls work, why do we still have the same problems after their use?

57.   Cracks are very common in eucalyptus trees in Australia.
       The trees are usually very strong compartmentalizers.
       However, the strong boundaries that resist the spread of
       decay following fire wounds are weak places where
       separations occur. These large meter squares of eucalyptus
       have many cracks that keep them from being used for high
       value products. The connection of fire wounds and cracks
       is not readily accepted in Australia.

701. Think about all the lucrative cures for Dutch elm disease. The trees still died.

702. Teaching is the most fulfilling and yet the most frustrating task in the world.

703. To open a closed mind is the highest reward for a teacher.

704. Product pushers come and go, teachers stay.

705. To start a person thinking is the same as starting a jet airplane. Now they can both fly.

706. Intelligence is the ability to make decisions that support high-quality survival.

707. Tree systems are intelligent. The messages in the DNA have "made" the best decisions for a long, high-quality life.

708. If people do not know who you are before they get to the lecture, no amount of introduction will change their feelings for you.

709. Trying to change the course of old Arboriculture is the same as trying to change the direction of the Queen Elizabeth II, in mud.

710. Nitrate and phosphate ions are Mack trucks. Ammonium and potassium cations are fast sports cars.

711. Fritz Haber, who discovered a way to synthesize ammonia, also discovered chlorine gas that killed thousands of Allied troops in World War I. When the gas was first used, his wife committed suicide. In 1919 Fritz Haber received a Nobel Prize for ammonia synthesis. At this time he had already been branded a war criminal.

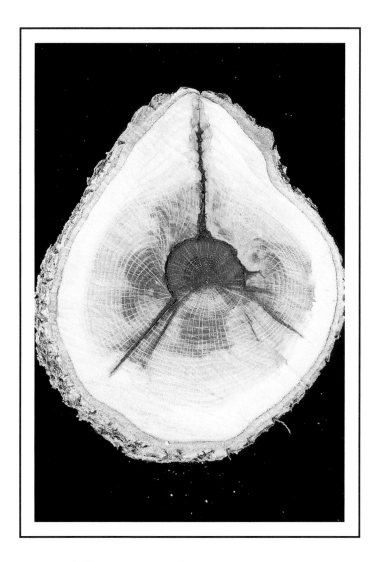

58. Cracks following wounding are shown in this white oak sample. The closure crack is above and the secondary cracks are at the five and seven o'clock positions. These cracks are often called frost cracks. The frost may trigger their spread after the stage is set by a wound.

712. Alfred Nobel became rich and famous because he saw the nitroglycerin seeping out of the clay, or kieselguhr, containers. He then incorporated nitroglycerin into a mixture of wood flour, ammonium nitrate, sulfur, and sodium nitrate to make dynamite. This was a safe way to handle a dangerous substance. (He also owned oil fields in Russia.)

713. Every time I meet another car at a remote intersection, I know Murphy's Law is alive and well.

714. Even the best batteries run down and need to be recharged.

715. A system that repeats itself will never perish.

716. Light connects the biotic and abiotic.

717. Why do we call them dumb animals when they know how to survive in the wild? Could you?

718. Think how many communities of life live on and in tree bark.

719. A brick will float when it has a wood board under it. Think what you can do when you make the right connections.

720. Most herbicides work by blocking enzymes.

721. Ticks, mites, and spiders are not insects. They are arachnids. They have eight legs.

722. When you are on a customer's property, talk briefly about some things you see that do not relate specifically with the reason for your being there. This will show that you have some credentials.

59.   Fractures are all too common on trees that have received flush pruning cuts and on trees where large sprouts grow on thin strips of sound wood as shown on this large old big-leaf maple.

723. Chitin is exactly the same as cellulose except in place of the OH group on the second carbon, there is an $NH(CO)CH_3$ group.

724. The exoskeletons of arthropods contain chitin.

725. Starch is an insoluble polysaccharide. It is made up of two glucose polymers, amylose and amylopectin. The glucose units are connected by 1-4 alpha linkages. Cellulose is connected by 1-4 beta linkages which causes the long molecule chain to twist.

726. Sucrose is a disaccharide made up of glucose and fructose.

727. About 65% of the sugars in maple sap are sucrose. That is why humans like it.

728. Trees produce many substances humans use for medicines. Some tree substances that contain nitrogen as a base are called alkaloids.

729. Quinine is an alkaloid from the bark of the cinchona tree. It is a treatment for malaria because it binds with DNA only in infected cells and prevents its replication.

730. The Neem tree native to India produces many substances valuable to humans.

731. What is a weed tree?

732. A child once asked me how a tree goes to the bathroom. Not an easy answer. Trees turn most of their products into substances that benefit the tree, such as extractives, crystals, and protection compounds. Trees have indoor plumbing. Living cells have vacuoles that collect products of metabolism. Animal cells do not have vacuoles.

60. Cracks and decay combined often form between squeezed
co-dominant stems. This red maple was dissected and
studied during an autopsy workshop. The only way to
understand internal defects is to dissect trees and to touch
all parts. People who have not done this should not talk
about trees.

733.   Anyone can put a tree in the ground. A few people know how to plant a tree correctly.

734.   Caring for a tree after it is planted is a long-term project not so different from education.

735.   Would it not be wonderful if all the people who get their pictures taken planting a tree were made responsible for the care of the tree?

736.   Many people have a very thin line between stimulation and irritation.

737.   The real "trick" or aim of teaching is to see how close you can get to the line of stimulation without crossing it into the zone of irritation.

738.   Teachers teach what they have been taught.

739.   Tolstoy said it best when he said that some people teach the same things so long that even when they are faced with overwhelming facts to the contrary, they will not change.

740.   Many highly intelligent people ran from high school biology and chemistry because of the ways they were taught. These people deserve another chance.

741.   Nature connects CHO in tens of thousands of compounds that all have different properties.

742.   Extracts from the bark of *Salix alba* were used by early humans to relieve pain. A much more purified form of the compound is called aspirin, one of the most commonly used analgesics in the world.

743.   Don't trust anybody who does not read the comics in the newspaper.

61. Wounds are all too common on trees growing in cities, parks, forests, and orchards. This young Monterey pine in New Zealand was wounded during a thinning operation. Note the thick woundwood that formed to the sides of the wound. Dissection shows clearly the growth history of the tree.

744. When I see some trees covered by mistletoe, I wonder which is the host and which is the parasite.

745. The Druids believed that the gods lived in the trees.

746. Before the United States was colonized, a squirrel could travel from Boston to St. Louis without touching the ground.

747. Hemlock trees will often be seen growing in straight lines in the forest because the seeds germinated on top of an old log. Hemlock seed rarely grows where there are old hemlock needles. This is also why large hemlock trees have prop-type roots. The seeds germinated on the cut stump of another tree.

748. I have examined many branches that fractured after the second or third loading. The first loading set the cracks and the second or third loading caused the final fracture.

749. Spider heart is a common feature in forest trees, especially white oaks. As the first crack forms, other cracks form that equalize the loading. Rarely will there be only one major crack or seam in a forest tree. Wetwood lubricates the cracks.

750. Cracks that start from the outer bark inward are usually very shallow. Large internal cracks start from weakened spots such as wounds, branch stubs, dead spots between co-dominant stems or roots, and insect wounds.

751. Cracks will never be understood from the transverse plane only. Longitudinal radial dissection must be made not only to understand cracks but other internal defects.

62.   Trees are often wounded by agents other than humans. Many trees in south Florida were injured severely by hurricane Andrew several years ago. After storm injury, work must be done first to reduce the risk of fractures that could cause problems for property and people. Next, the trees should be pruned for health. This means cutting off torn roots and removing long, injured branches to avoid sprouting that could lead to fractures.

752. All living things are bags of chemicals. Introduced other chemicals could benefit the bags – food – or disrupt the bags – poisons.

753. Chemical pathways are the routes traveled by chemicals in the bags. Shunts are detours. When trees are wounded, shunts produce protective substances.

754. People who say we know nothing about life are just not willing to learn.

755. Environment means collections of things about you. Natural systems mean connections of some of the things in ways so highly ordered that they repeat.

756. Knowledge is collections. Wisdom is connections.

757. The use of sex pheromones to trap insects is not fair!

758. An understanding of electrophysiology awaits us. Alteration of electromagnetic fields will confuse pathogens. This will be done by the people who escape from the cave.

759. In 1968 I saw convincing experiments showing the effects of electromagnetic fields on communications among termites. To show the effects, Prof. Dr. Günter Becker from Berlin said that you must first decrease the survival pressures on the termites.

760. When some event appears strange or "spooky" it only means, or proves, that we do not understand some natural phenomenon.

761. A true gardener will always pull some weeds while harvesting something from the garden.

63. In cold climates, winter ice injury can cause serious injuries. The same three part program given for hurricane injury should be done for ice-injured trees. In forests, the ice-injured trees add much needed carbon as cellulose for soil organisms. Forest practices during the last several decades have removed so much cellulose that I believe soil organisms are starving.

762. I have been convinced for many years that trees "carry" their own protective "wound dressings" in their bark. Now the same concept is being proved for human skin. A small protein called human beta-defensin-2 kills bacteria such as *Escherichia coli*, *Pseudomonas aeruginosa*, and the yeast *Candida albicans*. The skin antibiotic mechanically punches holes in the bacteria and yeast cells. A similar protein antibiotic exists in the human urogenital tract. My point. Once you learn just a little bit about biology and chemistry, you can read, understand, and enjoy the many journals now available to all.

763. Would you pay some doctor to reduce your defense systems?

764. The young vulture said to his mother, "Patience my behind, I'm going to kill something!!" I understand the feelings of the young bird when I see people injuring trees for money.

765. Any person can say, "I do not understand." It takes a very brave person to say, "Please help me to understand."

766. I have seen the best man could make for you and me. Then I went into the forest and touched a tree.

767. A successful business person once told me that researchers have all the answers but they don't know the questions.

768. The degree of effective management of any system is directly proportional to the degree of correct understanding of the system.

769. M and M people use their muscles and mind.

770. Learn to say money at least five times in your first sentence with a politician, and they may begin to listen.

64.   In spite of abiotic destructive forces and biotic agents such as insects, bacteria, and fungi, humans still rank as the major destructive agent for trees in forests and cities. Ignorance of tree biology is a major cause of this. Consider what people did to this walnut tree in California. The roots were trenched and treated, it was overfertilized, and the crown was overpruned. The tree is now mostly dead two years after treatments that had a very high price tag.

771. Natural systems are webworks. All parts are connected.

772. Truth is momentary perfect order.

773. Health is the ability to resist strain.

774. Vigor is the capacity to resist strain.

775. If you think you know something, write it and ask the person who reads it what you said. If the person does not receive what you said, maybe you really don't know what you thought you knew.

776. Dante will have a center chair waiting for tree mutilators.

777. Remember the dot-connecting games when you were a child? Some people must connect all the dots before they see the picture while others connect only a few.

778. Some people know a lot about animal tails, but they don't know which tails goes with which animal.

779. I have not been successful in catching a feeder root feeding under the microscope. I will keep up the search.

780. Why do some researchers delight in marching to near or distant drummers? Marching is a war thing mostly. We need more dances in research.

781. Why is it that complex answers are usually accepted before simple solutions?

782. Too many people talk too much about what they have not touched.

783. People want answers when solutions are needed. Answers are responses to questions. Solutions are responses to problems.

65.   If you think the last treatment was a crime, consider this one where several men spent several days wrapping this dying beech. It was dying because shallow roots were killed in attempts to establish a new lawn.

784. When the 17-year-locusts emerge, they bring a lot of nitrogen to the soil surface. When they die, their bodies fertilize the soil.

785. Botanists were often put on exploring ships to bring so-called magic plants back for the king's garden. This was a dangerous job because countries did not want their "magic plants" leaving their land.

786. Natural systems do not come in nice neat packages. Some parts always seem to "stick out" of the box.

787. As any job becomes more repetitious and follows simple repeating procedures, first the wages to do the job decrease, and then some machine is designed to do most or all of the job or the machines become robots. When people ask for recipes and lists, I know they are soon to be robots.

788. The more you do, the more the chances are that some errors will slip in.

789. Extremes cause rapid death. Living at the limits causes slow complicated death.

790. Membranes are nature's discriminators.

791. Science is a highly ordered collecting and connecting process. It is called often systematized knowledge. Science seeks to record what we think we know about life, the world, and the universe.

792. Why do people often say "<u>our</u> trees," "<u>our</u> world," "<u>our</u> forest," etc.? Who gave them to us? The philosophy of Native Americans was that the natural world belonged to all, and we were all responsible for its care. What happened to that?

66.   The last treatments shown were for payments. The crimes
       go on with acts that are difficult to understand, such as the
       killing of this large Douglas fir with golf tees. At least no
       one sent a bill. I keep thinking I've seen it all!

793. Don't sit in a 747 and criticize the Wright brothers!

794. No matter how big your house is, a good party will end with people crowded in the kitchen. This explains Van der Waals forces in chemistry. Atoms, as people, just like to cluster if they have the chance.

795. The little rich boy wanted a seesaw that only went up. No matter how rich you are, if you want to ride a seesaw you must be prepared to go down also.

796. Most so-called complex scientific theories and principles can be easily understood if they are explained by someone who really understands them.

797. Often we remember what we heard, but forget where we heard it. The unfair part is then to think it was original.

798. Too many philosophy books were written inside buildings.

799. When you ask a person a question and they respond by first using the word "well," you know they do not know. And, when you keep staring at them, they know, you know, they do not know.

800. The heart was thought to be the center for emotions. We still use it as meaning love. Too bad the center of a tree is called the heart. If any tree part should be called the heart, it should be the symplast.

801. Some people get the tree business and the business of trees confused.

802. Conflict of interest is becoming a serious problem in science where researchers benefit by saying very positive things about certain products.

67.   Trees do get their revenge.

803.   As any population increases, competition for survival also increases. Increasing populations often collapse not because of pressures outside their group but from pressures within the group.

804.   We need a natural philosophy that puts humans inside the system, not outside looking in.

805.   When nature comes up with something that works, it either multiplies it rapidly or makes it bigger.

806.   We need international chlorophyll day!

807.   Nurture and nature are Siamese twins.

808.   The people who say they do not need tree biology to do their job have a very strong case. One product kills all tree insects. Another product kills all disease-causing pathogens. What would you think of a doctor who had two treatments? How much would you pay the doctor?

809.   We are more dependent on trees than trees are on us.

810.   Lichens consist of fungi and algae. There are no data to show they harm trees.

811.   Pathogens are disseminated. Diseases are transmitted.

812.   Before women came to forestry, we called a tree or branch that was so weak that it could fall, a widow maker. Now what should we call them?

813.   If you will be had, you will be had!

814.   All large organisms in a doctor's waiting room will be the same genus and species – *Homo sapiens*. Tree people must deal with many genera of trees.

68.   Trees are not only the most forgiving living things on
      earth, they keep giving long after they die. We know they
      give their carbon and elements back to the earth for new
      organisms. Dead trees also provide many years of
      enjoyment for children. This tree fell after fungi rotted
      the roots. Children loved this tree in Auckland, New
      Zealand. It was pruned to make it safe and even a tire
      swing was added. Children love to climb trees and to
      touch trees. We should give them every opportunity to
      connect with nature.

815. People who say trees are just big plants should consider that you cannot fall out of a tomato plant, nor could one fall and kill a person!

816. Would it not be wonderful if we had a tree biology champion as well as a climbing champion?

817. As trees age, treatments should change, especially dose of fertilizers and pruning.

818. A young tree is 100% dynamic mass. This means that there are living cells every place there can be a living cell.

819. As the inner symplast dies, the dead expanding core becomes the static mass.

820. Ratios of dynamic mass to static mass should be the basis for dose of fertilizers and pruning.

821. A professional is a person who knows dose.

822. ATP is the "money" that runs people and trees.

823. Many processes and parts of human cells are not so different from those in trees.

824. Sooner or later most people become addicted to something. It could be a harmful or delightful addiction. Curiosity is a common addiction of some people.

825. Life must be dull and boring for people who know everything.

826. To know where you are going you must first know where you are now and how you got there.

827. The roots of arboriculture go deep within people who were not afraid of hard work for long hours.

69. Children of all ages like to play pretend. This tree in
    Bergen, Norway was the great dragon of the forest. We
    should give children more opportunities to play pretend
    by bringing selected safe trees into playgrounds.

828. Pruning, painting, and digging cavities were the icons of early arboriculture.

829. People who inject trees should be only those who understand, at the highest level, tree anatomy and physiology. (And I would like to give the test!)

830. In time, the muscle-only-arboriculture will separate from the muscle-and-mind-arboriculture.

831. The muscle-only arboriculture will never go away.

832. Customers come and go. Clients stay.

833. Understanding makes the complex simple.

834. Think about it! You are made up of chemicals that were parts of millions of other plants and animals. A product of recycling!

835. Needham may have been correct about spontaneous generation. I'm sure cardboard boxes are reproducing in the dark back corner of my garage.

836. People who do not believe over-pruning injures roots should be on the high end of a seesaw when the bottom person gets off suddenly.

837. You cannot buy credentials. They must be earned the old fashioned way.

838. The words "Line Clearing" must go! They have a very negative meaning, where lines are cleared at the expense of the trees. "Pruning near lines" or "utility pruning" should be the words.

839. Trees and their associates are living systems that respond with defense mechanisms to threats against their survival.

70.   This tree stump was the most photographed subject in this rose garden in Rome. I call such tree sections ecoart logs. They are beautiful. They connect with the soil and soil organisms. And, they give people a chance to touch and think about the wonders of our world. We need more ecoart logs in our landscapes. We have too many rocks.

840. Boundaries keep things together. Without them we would be blobs.

841. The rise of the middle class after the 1950's was a major factor affecting the growth of arboriculture.

842. Living processes seek the lowest energy state to do the work at the highest efficiency.

843. Waste is a human word for the product of inefficient management.

844. Plant lots of seeds – ideas – along the way. It is always surprising to see those that grow.

845. Pierre Balon, the first official botanist in France, was killed by a prowler. His friends knew he was killed because he knew too much about magic, medicinal plants and the ways they were traded. Joseph Pitton de Tournefort, also an early French botanist, was crushed against a wall by a large carriage. Again, his friends knew that his violent death was not an accident.

846. Real researchers record their data in ink, and their discussions in pencil.

847. Pathogens are well "designed" as thinning agents when populations get too crowded.

848. Leaders are people, or animals, that believe their mission is so important that they will continue on in spite of all odds.

849. Why is truth, so often, controversial, while myth is so acceptable?

850. When you keep pursuing a question in nature you, will always come to "I don't know."

71.   Palms are trees also. As trees they provide humans with many benefits. However, as trees they also receive some of the injuries other trees get from humans. Overpruning of palms can cause problems as constrictions in the trunk occur, and as the growing points are so weakened that opportunistic pathogens infect and sometimes kill the palms.

851. To stimulate is to start.

852. To motivate is to keep going.

853. If you want a large root system compared to the crown, top the tree.

854. When you look deep enough, in every person you will find a star.

855. People who have never dissected trees should not be allowed to talk about trees.

856. There is no product that will remedy ignorance.

857. Trees were here before people!

858. Buds are structures that are made up of embryonic shoots.

859. Meristematic points are radial clusters of parenchyma cells with "spear-like" points that are carried along in the bark.

860. When energy reserves decrease, meristematic points form sprouts.

861. Callose is a phloem polysaccharide. Callous means hardened. Callus is undifferentiated meristematic tissue.

862. Pathogens know how to wait.

863. Redox potential and the stock market are about the same thing — buying and selling or gaining electrons and using electrons.

864. Growth and maintenance are linked. Energy is required to maintain order in new mass.

865. To form bird's eye wood pattern, radial clusters of cambial cells dip inward as cones.

72. Trees do not move from place to place, but they move or sway constantly in place. The swaying can cause injured branches to weaken to the point of fracture. Small branches falling on people can cause serious problems. We look most of the time for overwhelming potential defects while the smaller defects are frequently overlooked.

866. Palms compartmentalize infected tissues.

867. People who haven't dug out tree roots or dissected trees should not be allowed to talk about trees.

868. "Next" is a frightening word when it means the next slide carousel.

869. Ideas persist when products perish.

870. Nature welcomes inquiry. Nature does not hide its work. Just seek, and you will find.

871. Wise people see also with their mind's eye.

872. Never underestimate the power of natural systems.

873. The sale of electronics and bottled water have been increasing at about the same rate. Maybe there is a message there.

874. The measure of real progress of any city or country is water in (you can drink it), water out (you can flush it safely), and trees (healthy, safe, attractive).

875. Ammonium ion has a molecular weight of 18 and potassium is 39, yet they are about the same size. This is important because they compete for space in some clay crystals.

876. Concentration gradients drive many processes.

877. Nature does not hide secrets! She pleads, and sometimes screams, for understanding.

878. Knowing chemistry will do little for the way tree care is practiced today.

73. In the beginning all organisms had "white hats." We thought all life forms were good or beneficial. As space and energy sources became limiting, some of the "good guys," the bonogens, took out the weaker members of the group. Because of the bonogens, the group survived. As humans came on the scene, the bonogens soon became the pathogens. The bonogens took out the London Plane leaves that grew from buds that had very little stored energy reserves. Now we call these fungi pathogens because "they cause" a disease we call anthracnose.

879. As the science of tree care develops, chemistry will become more important.

880. Remember: Recipes, Robots, Reduced Wages.

881. The mind must have not only an eye but also an ear. How else can it be explained that a deaf Beethoven could compose one of the grandest symphonies in the world that included the Ode to Joy chorus? (There is so much we don't understand.)

882. Nature gives us so much free, including mycorrhizae.

883. Forestry was founded on the basis of getting the wood out, not on understanding the tree.

884. Root rots kill trees by starvation. As the pathogens are compartmentalized, space for storage of energy reserves is reduced.

885. Having all the answers while inside is easy. Having the answers while working outside is not so easy.

886. It takes a big person to write a small book.

887. Did you hear about the people who wanted to ban dihydrogen oxide because they were told it caused many problems? Alas, they wanted to ban water!

888. As root hairs and mycorrhizae die, they add organic material to the soil.

889. Root hairs are extensions of single epidermal cells.

890. Chemistry connects anatomy and physiology.

891. An anonymous critic is the lowest form of life.

74.   Abiotic agents are still problems for trees. Lightning strikes cause all types of injuries from minor to fatal. There is no simple rule or answer to lightning injury. Every strike must be taken as a separate case. A problem is that it is difficult or impossible to design an experiment for the problem. The best that can be done is to watch the injured tree and to make certain it does not become a candidate for fracture.

892. Good stories live over and over again. They never die. Ask any child.

893. Root hairs and mycorrhizae are alive and well in midwinter in nonfrozen soils during warm spells and non-frozen soil below frozen soils.

894. The first settlers to America called trees their major enemy. It is time for forgiveness.

895. Ethics mean human behavior. Ethics could be bad, or good.

896. If a person says he or she understands trees, ask them how bark forms!

897. Stradivarius probably did not understand why, but he did use floated spruce that had bacterial erosion of pits for the bellies of his best violins.

898. Instrument builders usually know a great deal about building wood instruments but they know very little about the building material — wood.

899. Wood was a living material before it became a violin.

900. Wood characteristics start in the living tree.

901. Profits favor the wise.

902. I often wonder how much protoplasm the world can support.

903. Trees that grow in climates that have periods below $0°$ C do not freeze; they supercool.

904. At $40°$ below, Centigrade and Fahrenheit are the same.

75. The desire for trees in our cities goes on. The trees no
longer have the benefits of group defense and group
protection. Dutch elm disease is an example. The disease
in the natural stands did little harm. Actually, the fungi
and insects were more like bonogens than pathogens
because they served to maintain the self-thinning rule of
ecology. However, when elms were taken out of the
group and were not able to reproduce on concrete, their
defense and protection mechanisms were weakened. The
beneficial fungi and insects, the bonogens, were forced to
become pathogens. As more trees became trapped in
cities, the pathogens "had to" compete for the new energy
source. Then the pathogens did what they "knew" how to
do best: mutate and reproduce rapidly. Virulent forms
increased and soon even healthy trees were attacked. The
example is still Dutch elm disease. Think about it. We
have done the same for oak wilt and for many other
diseases in cities.

905. Isaac Newton is considered one of the most influential persons who ever lived.

906. Correct pruning cuts reduce the chances of at least 18 serious tree problems from happening.

907. The worst pruning I have ever seen has been in fruit tree orchards.

908. Pruning is a four part process; how to cut, which to cut, when to cut, and how much to cut. Not easy.

909. The degree of management of any system is directly proportional to the degree of understanding of the system.

910. Leaders get and give information. Others don't.

911. Remember, learn has earn in it. The more you learn the more you earn.

912. When power is out for over a week because of trees on power lines, people's ideas about trees and power lines change.

913. When you start with a false premise, you will always end with confusion!

914. The heartrot concept is based on the "fact" that wood is dead. And, that is not so. A false premise.

915. Short term experiments confuse more than confirm subjects.

916. When exotic plants are introduced into a new environment, their stay will be brief unless the environment is altered in ways that support their long-term survival.

76. "What is the answer?" Mrs. Mycorrhiza asks Mr. Mycorrhiza. It is time to learn some simple basics of tree biology. And, even some chemistry. The mere thought is enough to frighten many people. I remain optimistic. It will take at least another generation before these basic concepts become prerequisites for the title of arborist.

917. The increases in wood chipping industries say something about the quality of wood in many forest trees.

918. The focus of the Forest Products Laboratory that started in 1907 was on products, not on biology.

919. A healthy mature tree may have a thousand or more infections.

920. The theme of the tree system is perfect. We see only the variations which have many imperfections.

921. You cannot move to a higher comfort level without first passing through a level of discomfort.

922. Tree systems are like families. Families are made in ways that the members are connected in such highly ordered ways that high quality survival is ensured for all.

923. Too often cause and effect get mixed up.

924. Soils in the plains need carbon!

925. Myths start with a false premise.

926. Laugh out loud at least once a day. And this will keep the blues away.

927. Some people will buy products they do not understand and not buy books that will give them understanding.

928. If natural systems had not worked so well before we got here, we would never have gotten here.

929. Storms, fires, floods, earthquakes, and volcanic eruptions keep reminding us that we are not the boss.

930. Trees do not move from place to place, but they are constantly moving in place.

77.   This is where some tree people are today. I am quick to say that there are an increasing number of exceptions, or people who know it is time to use our minds as well as our muscles. Hard work will always be a part of arboriculture. The marketplace demands better, faster, and less expensive service. I remain optimistic.

931. The first microorganisms that infect fresh chips are those that digest the defenseless cell contents.

932. Bark contains suberin, which is cork. Cork resists breakdown by microorganisms.

933. Bark mulch may alter soil structure but the bark does not add carbon to the soil.

934. As trees age, emphasis should go from health, to beauty, to safety.

935. After storm injury, cut for safety first. If possible, leave long stubs so correct cuts can be made when there is more time.

936. Trees have many bark diseases that are poorly understood.

937. Aerial roots become prop roots when they anchor in the soil.

938. Natural successions are orderly sequences of organisms that either build up or break down living systems.

939. *Phialophora* species are well adapted with their phialides for sporulation within trees because the phialides produce spores in confined spaces.

940. Yeasts are fungi.

941. Paradoxical effects mean that as dose increases the response is increasing and decreasing as an undulating wave between an x and y axis.

942. Root sprouts come from meristematic points in roots. Roots do not have buds.

78.   Life is a journey, powered by the sun, of a highly ordered and connected group of chemicals borrowed from the earth.

Death is the end of the journey where the borrowed chemicals are returned to the earth to be used again for new life.

943. Green is the dominant color of nature, yet green was one of the last fabric stains invented by man.

944. "Nature and nature's laws lay hid in night: God said, Let Newton be! and all was light."   Alexander Pope

945. Opera and nature are similar in that the whole is greater than the sum of the parts.

946. "God wrote two books, the scriptures and nature," said Galileo. To read nature you must connect with it; touch it.

947. Boredom is the major cause of accidents in arboriculture.

948. Glyphosate kills by disrupting the shikimic acid pathway in plants. Fungi also have the same pathway.

949. Vandals destroy without seeking payment. What do you call a person who destroys trees and still wants payment for doing it?

950. **Ignorance of tree biology has been, and still is, the major cause of tree problems worldwide.**

To survive,

keep your message simple,

and repeat it!

To survive,

keep your message simple,

and repeat it!

TOUCH TREES

FOR MUCH MORE ON ALL SUBJECTS GIVEN HERE, SEE
TREE EDUCATIONAL MATERIALS
BY
DR. ALEX L. SHIGO
SHIGO AND TREES, ASSOCIATES
P.O. BOX 769
DURHAM, NH 03824-0769   USA
PHONE 603 868 7459   FAX 603 868 1045

ORDER
CODE

BOOKS

A. **A NEW TREE BIOLOGY** — hard cover, 619 pages and **DICTIONARY** soft cover, 132 pages. (Sold only as a set).

H. **TREE PRUNING** — hard cover, 127 full-color photos, 192 pages.

M. **MODERN ARBORICULTURE** — hard cover, 311 diagrams, 16 photos, 440 pages.

F. **ARBORICULTURA MODERNA COMPENDIO** — soft cover, 160 pages, Spanish.

R. **100 TREE MYTHS** — soft cover, 80 pages, 100 myths, 26 near myths.

S. **TREE ANATOMY** — hard cover, 104 pages, micro views, 94 large full-color photos.

VIDEO

Q. **A CLOSER LOOK AT TREES** — 2 hour video under a low power microscope.

SLIDE PACKAGES

J. **TREE PRUNING slides** — 125 color slides from the book, with script.

N. **MODERN ARBORICULTURE slides** — 120 new color slides and script.

T. **TREE ANATOMY, BELOW GROUND** — 80 color slides, script, and audio tape.

U. **TREE ANATOMY, ABOVE GROUND** — 80 color slides, script, and audio tape.

BOOKLETS, BROCHURES, PAMPHLETS and POSTERS

D. **NEW TREE HEALTH** — 12 page full color booklet.

L. **CARING FOR YOUNG TREES** — 12 panel color brochures.

K. **PRUNING TREES NEAR ELECTRIC UTILITY LINES** — a field pocket guide.

O. **5 MINUTE TREE CARE** — 8 page booklet, red and green, diagrams.

E. **TREE HAZARDS** — 10 panel fold-out brochure, 13 diagrams.